Spirit of India

Spirit of India

APJ Abdul Kalam

rajpal

Price: One Hundred Ninety Five only (Rs. 195/-)

Edition: 2010 © APJ Abdul Kalam

ISBN: 978-81-7028-795-7

Spirit of India by APJ Abdul Kalam

Rajpal & Sons, Madarsa Road, Kashmere Gate, Delhi 110006

www.rajpalpublishing.com

email : mail@rajpalpublishing.com

Contents

Spirit of India

The independence movement created and nurtured the concept that the nation is bigger than any individual or any system of organisation. But during the last few decades this national spirit has been at a low ebb. What we need today is that all political parties co-operate with one another and answer the overwhelming question facing all of us : "When will India become a developed nation?"

There has to be unflinching commitment to the principle of secularism, which is the cornerstone of our nationhood and which is the key feature of our civilisational strength. Leaders of all religions should echo one message, that of unity of the minds and hearts of our people, and soon we will see the golden age of our country.

The need of the hour is disciplined action by all citizens. This will lead to the creation of enlightened citizens. Any country is as good as its citizens. Their ethos, their values and their character will be reflected in the country's make-up. These are crucial factors that will determine whether the country will move forward on a progressive path or stagnate.

All of us have to practise the values of honesty, sincerity, discipline and tolerance in our day-to-day living. This will elevate our politics to statesmanship. We have to collectively inculcate a positive attitude of what we can do for our country so that together we will be able to benefit ourselves.

We have immensely benefited from what our ancestors did and left for us. We have a right and responsibility to leave a positive legacy to posterity for which we all will be remembered.

If the 540 million youth work with the spirit "I can do it", "we can do it" and "India can do it" nothing can stop India from becoming a developed country

What is of vital importance – personal development or national development? In what way does personal development contribute to national development?

Heeba Jemi, Lady Doak College, Madurai

National development has to be achieved through people. Hence, development of people is very important. We have to create a personal development programme which will create enlightened citizens who in turn will contribute towards national development.

In your opinion, who serves the country best – a soldier,
a teacher, a doctor, a scientist or a politician?

Tarannum, Kendriya Vidyalaya, Pathankot

All have their own role to play to serve the country in
the best possible way.

A soldier has to defend the nation and keep
round-the-clock vigil so that the billion plus people
can work towards development in peace.

A teacher has to create enlightened citizens and future
leaders.

'Use your brain to remove the pain of suffering
humanity' should be the motto of doctors.

Scientists should provide the inputs needed for
achieving development.

Politicians have to integrate and guide the actions of
all sections of the community towards a common
goal of national development.

And above all one has to be a good human being.

What can be the role of a common man in your vision of a developed India?

Lal Mani Vikas Bharati, Munger

A common man can educate those who cannot read and write, plant trees in his neighbourhood and maintain them, enable upkeep of the place where he lives and its surroundings, and also report certain undesirable things which are against the interest of the nation to the authorities.

What is the greatest obstacle which is preventing India from becoming a developed nation?

David P. Kahn, Connecticut College, USA

Our defeatist tendency is the greatest obstacle in our march towards becoming a developed nation. Having a low aim is also a big obstacle. In fact, it is a crime to have a low aim. Once our people are enthused with the ambition of high aims everything else will fall into place. And to lead the people we need mission-oriented leaders with great leadership qualities.

With great power comes great responsibility. What do you think individual citizens should do to contribute in making our society and country more responsible?

Arjun Nair, Kochi

All the citizens must realise their individual responsibilities and perform their duties, in whatever area they are, with commitment and devotion. By setting an example they will generate a sense of responsibility and commitment amongst the younger generation.

We see that individualism is defeating nationalism and because of this our country is not able to progress much. What effective measures can be taken to prevent this?

Shubham Das, Howrah

I feel that the spirit of nationalism was very strong when India was vigorously pursuing its freedom movement from 1857 to 1947. A similar spirit was noticed whenever India was facing conflicts or war on its borders. It looks to me that now we need a second vision for the nation, just like when we were actively pursuing our freedom movement against alien rule. This second vision for making India a developed nation will bring the spirit of nationalism to the fore.

We celebrate our national days with great fervour, solidarity and patriotism but the very next day selfish concerns overshadow our national interests. Why is this so and what can we do to change it?

Esha Mahindru, DAV School

We have to convert every celebration of our national days into a societal mission of being useful to the society. On each of these occasions we should ask ourselves the question, "What can I give?" and act accordingly. Giving makes the giver happy and also the needy receiver happy. This process has to be cultivated in homes and schools. If this is done, working for national interest without any selfish motive will become the habit of our youth.

It has been sixty-two long years that India has been free—socially, economically and politically but what disheartens me is that as yet India has not been able to attain stability. Where exactly did we go wrong?

Ankit Arvind, Apeejay School, Noida

India is progressing and is on a continuous growth path. When you move forward a certain amount of instability will always be there. We have to overcome the instability and move forward with determination. As in the case of a fighter aircraft flying at Mach 3 speed, the structure is always made slightly unstable so as to absorb any unforeseen events or pressures.

*If a SWOT (strength, weakness, opportunity, threat)
analysis is done for India, what do you think would be
the outcome?*

Jayajanani Pattabhiraman, VJTI, Mumbai

Our strength—a large biodiversity and large pool of
human resource.
Weakness–self-doubt.
Opportunity—a large market of 300 to 400 million
people in the middle income group.
Threat—competition from some of the countries in
the region and maintenance of ecological balance.

*What is the main factor that made India so prosperous
at one time and which is lacking today?*

Srushti Susarla, Sanskriti School, Pune

'Work with integrity and succeed with integrity'
— that is missing today.

Spirit of India

Our inability to address inequality and cultural chauvinism has led to the emergence of new forms of exclusion which threatens the social fabric of India which is marked by diversity. How can a democratic people address this critical concern?

Usman Javed, St. Xavier's College, Mumbai

I would like to recall an incident from my childhood. When I was a young boy of ten years I would see three unique personalities meet in our house. They were Pakshi Lakshmana Shastrigal, who was the head-priest of the famous Rameswaram temple and a great Vedic scholar, Rev. Father Bodal, who built the first church in Rameswaram island and my father who was an Imam in the mosque. All three of them would sit together and discuss the island's problems and try to find solutions. Their interaction helped build connectivity amongst the people of different religions and the effect of this spread to others on the island like fragrance from flowers. The memory of this meeting always comes to my mind whenever I discuss with people about the need for having dialogue amongst different religions. India has had this unique advantage of integration of minds for thousands of years. This has to be strengthened. In our own way, we have created a foundation called FUREC (Foundation for Unity of Religions and Enlightened Citizenship) which has members from fifteen different faiths in the country. We need many more such institutions for promoting unity of minds.

What kind of policy will help in the development of the economy of India?

Priyanka Bakshi, C.N.I. Girls Inter College, Dehradun

We have to maintain a balanced development between rural India and urban India. We should create a knowledge society using our core competence in various sectors such as ICT (information and communication technology) and biotechnology. For rapid economic development it is essential that a citizen-centric approach to evolution of business policy, creation of young and dynamic leaders, user-driven technology generation and intensified industry-laboratory-academy linkages become our focus areas.

With so much wealth and talent, why is India still not considered a developed nation?

Mansi Shah, Ahmedabad

Even though we have wealth and talent in certain areas, we still have 260 million people below the poverty line. We can become a developed nation as soon as we can uplift these 260 million people to prosperity through our hard work and determination. Then India will become a prosperous, peaceful and happy state.

*How can we build a dynamic India given the prevalent
conditions of unemployment, poverty and corruption?*

Piyush Srivastava, Indian Institute of Information Technology, Allahabad

Education has to be the first priority. Education must
lead to the creation of job-providers rather than
job-seekers. We should try to create a large number
of non-farm rural enterprises which can provide
employment to people in the rural sector.

*India has more millionaires than some of the European
countries and also many more shivering beggars on
traffic signals than anywhere else in the world. Why?*

Kavya Chaturvedi, Delhi Public School, Noida

What is needed is inclusive growth. Till now most
of the development has been taking place in urban
India. This has to be extended to rural India where
700 million people live in 600,000 villages. Though
the number of people below the poverty line has
come down during the last few years, with greater
development momentum and emphasis on agriculture
and agro-processing, I am sure we will soon be able to
eradicate poverty from our country.

How do you visualise India in the year 2020?

Shefali Singh, SS Khanna Girls Degree College, Allahabad

I have a ten-point distinctive profile for a developed India :

- A nation where the rural and urban divide has been reduced to a thin line
- A nation where there is an equitable distribution of resources and adequate access to energy and quality water
- A nation where agriculture, industry and service sector work together in symphony
- A nation where education with value system is not denied to any meritorious candidate because of societal or economic discrimination
- A nation which is the best destination for the most talented scholars, scientists, and investors
- A nation where the best health care is available to all
- A nation where the governance is responsive, transparent and corruption-free
- A nation where poverty has been totally eradicated, illiteracy removed and crimes against women and children are absent and none in the society feels alienated
- A nation that is prosperous, healthy, secure, devoid of terrorism, peaceful and happy and progresses on a sustainable growth path
- A nation that is one of the best places to live in and is proud of its leadership.

How can I choose the right person in elections?

Vijayan, Vettavalam, Tiruvannamala Dist.

In my view, nobility of the candidate (or righteousness of the candidate) and performance in the constituency has to be the criteria.

Inequality of income,
greed to possess
whatever is possible,
non-consideration of the
problems of other people
are some of the causes
of corruption

In today's world, India's civilisation values appear to be more on paper than in spirit. Corruption is rampant, basic amenities are still denied to the majority of the population, poor administration and lack of ethics in political governance has become a national curse. Despite a rich cultural heritage and civilisation from which we can draw lessons, how have we reached this situation? Have our civilisational ethos failed us?

Capt. Chadha, Naval Higher Command Course, Mumbai

Inspite of all these shortcomings, India is functioning as the largest stable democracy in the world. Within this democratic setting we can find solutions to all the problems in a progressive manner. What we need to do, is to ignite the minds of the youth with good thoughts, so that they can dream big and achieve great things.

Have our civilisation values turned us into a soft state? We seem to accept all atrocities but are unable to deliver a decisive reply as evident in our dealings with terrorism or piracy?

Capt. Beecha, Naval Higher Command Course, Mumbai

The way to combat any organised threat to society is through unity of people and purpose. "When evil minds combine, good minds have to work together to combat."

Why are we forgiving Pakistan, even though they send terrorists to India?

Faiz, R.P.V.V., Tyagraj Nagar, Delhi

We want an environment of external peace so that our economic development is fast and our people living below the poverty line can get a good life. Peace in South Asia will also benefit the region as a whole as poverty is our common enemy.

As India is rapidly advancing forward, we have large disparities amongst our people – both in terms of wealth and perspectives. Amongst rising aspirations which drive our forward movement, and unfulfilled expectations which push us back and apart, how do we balance this divergence?

Capt. G.K. Garg, Naval Higher Command Course, Mumbai

Education has to be the first priority and must lead to the creation of job-providers rather than job-seekers. We should try to create large numbers of non-farm rural enterprises which can provide employment to people in the rural sector.

*You have written a book about India's futuristic
ambitions i.e. "India 2020". What inspired you to think
so deeply? Do you think India will be able to achieve
the aims you have set inspite of all the problems we are
facing?*

Himani, Apeejay School, Jalandhar

"India 2020" was the outcome of a project undertaken
by the Technology Information and Forecasting
Council of the Department of Science and
Technology in 1997. I happened to be the Chairman
of the Council at that time. We mobilized over five
hundred specialists from different fields and generated
a blueprint for "India 2020". The Indian economy
is a large economy of around one billion people.
Anything which we attempt to do needs a time lag for
yielding results. That is the reason we took a 20 year
lead time and chose the year 2020 when India would
be transformed into a developed nation. India is well
on its way to accomplish the target. Our younger
generation must have the spirit of "I can do it".
That will ensure our accomplishing the goals of
"India 2020".

Our poet says there is no caste or community in the society. But, in day-to-day life, wherever we go we have to mention these things. Why is this so? How do we find a solution for this?

K. Bindhu, Pondicherry Institute of Hotel Management and Catering, Pondicherry

A borderless society with no divisions of caste and community can only arise from borderless minds. It has taken centuries for our society to evolve into the present structure of caste and community. Love, patience, good laws and fair justice are the best instruments for our society to transform itself into a borderless community where 'hands that serve are better than lips that pray.'

Houses, villages, districts, states and countries have tensions on the issue of boundaries. Aquifers, rivers, animals and humans do not obey borders. Can we live in a world without boundaries or borders?

Lohit Sarangi, Jyoti Vihar High School

The moment all of us become givers and not takers, we will be in a position to live in a world without boundaries or borders.

How can we eradicate terrorism?

Devesheesh Bose, Bhopal

Terrorism is caused due to instability in the social structure. If we can provide adequate employment opportunity to the youth and remove the imbalanced distribution of wealth, terrorism can be eradicated.

What are the methods that we need to adopt to have a more transparent and efficient political system?

Rishanaka Bawa, Kamla Nehru College, New Delhi

Development must be the focus irrespective of party affiliations. The electorate should choose those candidates who can deliver results towards the development of their constituency with efficiency and transparency. To enable any nationally-oriented person to enter the electoral process, the funding of elections by the government has to be explored. Technology has to be used to improve visibility of performance of development programmes and services, so that the citizens are aware of all actions taken by the political system.

How do you justify the statement, preparation for war as a defence for peace?

My view on this is as follows : For the last three thousand years India has been invaded by many countries. Alexander invaded India, the French, Dutch and Portugese set up their colonies in our country and then we were ruled by the British. Why?

India needs peace for its progress. When all around us, our neighbouring countries have nuclear weapons India cannot sit and do *tapas*. Strength respects strength. Whatever we have done in defence is only to defend our freedom. At no time either in the past or in the future would India ever invade any nation. Our nuclear policy enunciates no-first-use. That means defending the country is the foremost mission.

*How is your "Vision 2020" related to
the progress of our country?*

Gulfishan, Jamia Senior Secondary School, Delhi

"Vision 2020" is aimed at creating
a poverty-free India. For that,
our GDP has to be increased to
10% per annum and maintained
at that level for a decade. For
this, we need to have a roadmap
focussing on five areas: agriculture
and food processing; education
and healthcare; information and
communication technology; reliable
and quality electric power, surface
transport and infrastructure for
all parts of the country; and self-
reliance in critical technologies.
These five areas are closely inter-
related and if developed in a
coordinated way, will lead to food,
economic and national security.

*Terrorism is caused
due to instability in the
social structure. If we
can provide adequate
employment opportunity
to the youth and
remove the imbalanced
distribution of wealth
terrorism can be
eradicated*

As a leader of a billion people what, in your experience, is that one thing that can inspire people to put the nation's interest ahead of their own interest?

Student, Wharton Business School
University of Pennsylvania, USA

It is a beautiful question. It is the quality of leadership that can inspire people to consider the nation ahead of their own interest. A leader who can absorb and take responsibility for the failures and give credit for success to his team will be able to inspire his people.

36

Spirit of India

I am an eight year old girl residing in a remote place of Jharkhand where frequent incidents of violence take place. I think that "corruption" and "faith of distorted philosophy" is the reason behind this act of terror. What is the government doing to eradicate corruption from our society?

Riya Sinha, Ursuline Convent School, Ranchi

I believe corruption in the society can be eliminated in two ways. One, we elect the right representatives to legislatures and parliament. Two, corruption-free society starts from a righteous home. In my view corruption can be eliminated only by three people, namely mother, father and elementary school teacher. As children you can point out if anything wrong is done in your home. There will definitely be a change because of the love and affection of the child.

How can we say that India is a true democracy when there are fifteen or sixteen parties which contest in the elections?

Ayush Kala, C.N.I. Boys Inter College, Dehradun

This is the very beauty of democracy that there is unity as well as diversity. All individuals have a right to follow the path which they consider best. As the nation gets developed, finally what will emerge will be a two-party system.

What do you think India will be like after a hundred years from today?

Sukumar, Ahlcon Public School, New Delhi

I feel it will be characterised by three major features: One, it will have a strong and powerful educational system like what we had more than a thousand years ago in Nalanda in Bihar. The research potential of our educational institutions will attract foreigners to India. Two, the earth's resources will be exhausted. There will therefore be big satellites in the earth's orbit that will supply solar energy through microwave. Three, the human race will establish a habitat on Mars. Maybe some of you will live there!

What role can globalisation play in the development of rural India?

Varun Srivastava, MGR Educational & Research Institute, Chennai

Globalisation plays an important role in overall development of the economy as it promotes competitiveness. If our industries can use rural India for developing and producing knowledge products, Indian products can become more competitive in the international market. This will eventually aid employment generation in the rural sector and increase the pace of development in rural India.

Spirit of India

How are we to reconcile globalisation, privatisation, economic reforms on the one hand and increasing population and unemployment on the other?

Abhishek S. Deshpande, Singrur

Globalisation, privatisation and economic reforms have started paying off. As you are aware, our GDP (gross domestic product) has started growing at around 7 to 8 per cent. Agriculture, manufacturing and service industries are all on an ascent phase. This is the phase in which we will see large scale growth in employment opportunities. In addition, the recently approved PURA (Providing Urban Amenities in Rural Areas) programme by the government and the growing service sector will create both entrepreneurial and employment opportunities for the rural population.

What are your views on foreign investment in Indian trade and business?

*Pankaj Srivastav, Wharton Business School
University of Pennsylvania, USA*

We welcome foreign investment as long as it leads to a win-win situation for both. The problem comes when you have a win-lose situation.

In the context of the present day globalised world, is it not that government intervention and public sector are subordinated to the private sector? But at the same time, governmental and public sector responsibilities for social good cannot be underestimated. What is your opinion on this?

Kunal Kumbhat, National Law University, Jodhpur

In a globalised world, government, public sector and private sector all have to work as partners to make the country economically competitive. No one is superior or inferior. All have to play their role. All of them must remember that the nation is above any one individual or organisation.

*Are you a champion of 'Sarva Dharma' society?
Is harmony of religions a dream or a reality?*

Rohit Mishra, J.S.S. Medical College, Mysore

Yes. Religions are veritable islands. If we connect all the religions through love and compassion, we will definitely have religious harmony and lasting peace.

*One of India's strength has been its spirituality. What
is your advice on retaining spirituality as our country
progresses and becomes more materialistic?*

*Balaji Thiagarajan, Wharton Business School
University of Pennsylvania, USA*

One of our strengths is our joint family system. In this
system a problem is no problem whereas in a nuclear
family a problem can destroy a family. We have a
number of religions. I find that religions are like
orchards, but they need to be linked. Every religion
preaches compassion and love. If we can transform
religion into a spiritual force then we have arrived.

*India is a multi-lingual and multi-racial country with
many religions. Do you agree that unity among the
people of the country is most important and how will we
achieve it?*

Subhajit Ganguli, Kolkata

Harmony comes from tolerance. We should cultivate a
sense of unity amidst diversity of region, religion and
language. These divisive forces should be converged
as cohesive forces for bringing about peace in the
society. Nation is bigger than any individual, religion
or organisation. If we keep this in mind and work
together there will be unity among all our people.

A borderless society with no divisions of caste and community can only arise from borderless minds

In recent years, the enemy from within seems to be becoming more powerful than the enemy without, and providing opportunities for otherwise weaker external enemies. This is mirrored in our civilisational history, which has seen so many cases of our own people collaborating with the enemy and this has been the cause of our collective downfall. What, in your view, is the reason for this lacunae in our civilisation and how do we overcome it?

Capt. Virender Kumar, Naval Higher Command Course, Mumbai

History has found that we have always been defeated by the enemy within. To remove the enemy within we have to have a righteous heart as reflected in the following hymn :
Where there is righteousness in the heart
There is beauty in the character,
When there is beauty in the character
There is harmony in the home,
When there is harmony in the home
There is order in the nation,
When there is order in the nation
There is peace in the world.

There is a beautiful connectivity between heart, character, nation and the world. In a society we have to build righteousness among all its constituents. For the society as a whole to be righteous we need creation of righteousness in family, righteousness in education, righteousness in service, righteousness in career, righteousness in business and industry, righteousness in civil administration, righteousness in politics, righteousness in government, righteousness in law and order, righteousness in justice.

In addition to inculcating righteousness in all aspects of society, indomitable spirit is essential for realizing the vision of a developed India.

How relevant in the consumer era of today is the 'Nishkam Karmayog' philosophy of "Bhagvad Gita?"

Navdha Pandey, Uttaranchal Sanskrit Academy, Dehradun

The teachings of *Gita* are relevant for all times. *Nishkam Karma* will always ensure peace and prosperity to the individual, family, society and the nation. Selfishness will only lead to distress and destruction.

The collective thought
of channellised powerful
minds is the real strength
of any nation

There is a certain lack of sense of ownership in public affairs in India. The concept that something belongs to the 'Sarkar' is instinctively viewed as something that is feudal and exploitive. The lack of an inclusive sense of collective ownership in public affairs is perhaps an inheritance from the feudal sections of our history. How does modern India free itself from the yoke of caste, feudalism, and parochialism, and where, if at all, do our civilisational values help us to counter this aspect of our civilisational baggage?

Capt. O Johnson, Naval Higher Command Course, Mumbai

Our civilisational values have always been preaching that we should be unselfish and try to help remove others' pain. This comes out of training in the home and school.

Here, I am reminded of the advice given to Mahatma Gandhi by his mother. She said, "Son, in your entire life time, if you can save or better someone's life, your birth as a human being and your life is a success. You have the blessing of the Almighty God."

This advice made a deep impact on the mind of Gandhiji, and inspired him to work for the cause of humanity throughout his life. This advice should be followed by every citizen of India.

How can India become the knowledge powerhouse of the world and how would this help in eradicating poverty from India and the world?

Shamsher Singh,
Indian Institute of Information Technology, Allahabad

India has to graduate from being an industrial economy to becoming a knowledge economy with emphasis on empowerment of the people besides providing basic needs for all-round development. The education system has to be creative, interactive, self-learning and informal with focus on values, merit and quality instead of being just text-book based teaching. Workers have to be flexibly skilled, knowledgeable and self-empowered instead of being merely categorized as skilled or semi-skilled. The type of work will be less structured and software-driven instead of being structured and hardware-driven. Management will be more delegative instead of being directive. And the negative impact on environment and energy will be strikingly less.

The Taj Mahal, Bhakra Nangal Dam, Agni-III missile, which is more important for India?

Munisa Tanveer, Madina School, Hyderabad

The Taj Mahal is an embodiment of artistic beauty. The Bhakra Nangal Dam leads to economic growth. Agni-III is required for defending the nation. You cannot eliminate or substitute one for the other.

Spirit of India

The threat of violence has restricted any meaningful exercise of the right to freedom of speech and expression. In your view, should there be any limits or restrictions on the exercise of this right? If so, on what grounds?

Manashi Parashar,Indraprastha College for Women, Delhi

People should not be afraid of violence. Violence has to be tackled in its own way. People should have the right to freely express their views as that is fundamental to the functioning of democracy.

Why there is so much corruption in the country?

Sandeep Upadhyaya, Indore

Inequality of income, greed to possess whatever is possible, non-consideration of the problems of other people are some of the causes for corruption.

*Can India and Pakistan ever come to mutual
understanding on the issue of Kashmir?*

Abhijit Singh, DAV Institute of Engineering and Technology, Jalandhar

Let us look at two examples from history.

The European nations were fighting with each other
for centuries and even caused the two world wars.
Today, twenty-seven countries of Europe have joined
hands and formed the European Union and have
a common Parliament to govern their collective
economic development while ensuring prosperity of
the individual nations.

USA and the erstwhile USSR were at 'cold war' with
each other for nearly fifty years and each accumulated
tens of thousands of nuclear warheads. Today, they
are sitting across the table with each other and talking
about world peace.

This just goes to show that with changing situations
the relationship between nations can also change.

What is the role of human values and culture in transforming India into a developed nation? And what steps can an individual take in his day-to-day living to achieve this?

Sudhir, Indian Institute of Science, Bangalore

Righteousness is the key value to be followed for transforming India into a developed nation. For enabling righteousness to percolate among the masses, youth must take the responsibility of influencing their parents and making the family righteous. If youth can undertake this task I am sure the entire country will become righteous and India will soon be a developed nation.

Why don't people live peacefully?
People are constantly fighting over
'mandir-masjid', can't you do
something about it? Can't you pass
laws or impose rules to make this world
worth living? Please comment.

Sara and Ali, All Saints and Sherwood College, Nainital

Under-developed minds normally
create differences. Developed
minds create visions and differences
disappear.

Spirit of Education

Education transforms a human being into a wholesome whole, a noble soul and an asset to the universe. Real education enhances the dignity of a human being and increases his or her self-respect and promotes universal brotherhood.

Education in its real sense is the pursuit of truth with the teacher in the pivotal position who has to continuously replenish and update his knowledge so that his wards will always look up to him as a walking encyclopaedia, as a fountain of love and, most of all, a caring human being.

If only the real sense of education could be realised by each individual with the guidance of the teacher, and carried forward in every field of human activity the world will be so much a better place to live in.

Today's young students want the education system to feed and challenge their innovative and creative minds. They are the creators of tomorrow and they want to think about it today. A good system of education should be able to satisfy their insatiable hunger for knowledge.

Educational institutions have to gear up to evolve a curriculum that is sensitive to the social and technological needs of a developed India. Student activities towards development should be seamlessly integrated with the existing curriculum so that the future members of our society are fully devleoped in all aspects of societal transformation.

What really is education? Is education just about reading books or going to school? Or is it about acquiring knowledge?

Anuj Goel, La Martiniere Girls College, Lucknow

The goal of education is to create an enlightened society.

Enlightened society has three components. One, education with value system, two, religion transforming into spiritual force and three, economic development. Going to school must empower the youth to become a part of the knowledge society and contribute to the national development apart from their own growth.

How much time should one devote for becoming a good student?

D.N. Joshi, Kendriya Vidyalaya, Almora

A good student arrives when his learning process takes care of two aspects : one is knowledge acquisition and the other is acquisition of good value system.

Don't you think the present generation is over-burdened; they face pressure from parents and teachers to perform well in school. In what way can you help the children to cope with this situation?

Master Dewang Pandey, Sandipani, Nagpur

Yes, whenever I meet parents and teachers I suggest that it is very important that the children are given freedom to select the subject of their choice after 10+2. This is an important parental contribution to the children's growth. Of course, the children have the responsibility to hear their inner conscience about their genuine aptitude in the subject and not be governed by opinion of friends and colleagues.

There are so many distractions today. How can we overcome these and develop ourselves to become responsible students?

S. Lakshmi, St. Sri Sankara Mat. Hr. Sec. School Thiruvanmiyur, Chennai

Distractions are part of life. As responsible students, you have to recognise your strengths and interests. Select a goal, work hard and succeed. While working to achieve the goal you will definitely encounter some problems but you should not be defeated by them. You should defeat the defeatist tendency and excel in your mission. That is how you can succeed in your life.

On the one hand we are talking about bringing 100%
literacy in the country. On the other hand, education is
becoming more expensive. How can a rational balance be
brought about between the two?

Yagika, Shree Kasturba High School, Rajkot

There is a need to improve the quality of education
in the state-run schools where the cost of education is
fairly low. For improving the quality of education, we
have to use modern technology backed by few good
teachers and the dissemination has to take place with
the use of tele-education. This is a good investment
which should be met from the government budget.
Also, students of higher classes should teach the lower
class students, without any charge.

Besides education, what are the other things which you
think are necessary for schools to impart to students so
as to help them face the challenges of the world and be a
better citizen of the country?

Apoorva Sundaram, Jaya Jaya Sankara International School
Nazarathpet, Chennai

A school must provide an opportunity for developing
a multi-faceted personality of the students, such as
proficiency in games, debating, entrepreneurship,
development of cultural values and so on and these
activities must become part of the school curriculum.

*My idea of education
is to bring out the
creativity of the
individual*

Do you think that there is a link between our existing education system and real life?

N. Pavithra, Jaycees Matriculation, Higher Secondary School, Erode Distt,

There should be a link between the existing education system and real life. To keep pace with the changes in real life, our education system is being constantly upgraded to prepare the students with capacities such as research and enquiry, creativity and innovation, use of the latest technology, entrepreneurial leadership and moral leadership. All these capacities are needed for facing the realities of life.

How can we develop our vision so that education does not serve the purpose of only earning bread and butter? How can it produce moral leaders of tomorrow?

Yogesh Kumar Mishra, Banaras Hindu University, Varanasi

The education system must concentrate on developing five types of minds in an individual, namely: disciplined mind, synthesizing mind, creative mind, respecting mind and ethical mind. The first three minds deal with the individual and the last two deal with the relationship of the individual to a group or society. A harmonious mix is needed between the two to develop moral leaders. In other words, the education system must focus on creating all the five types of mind in students so that they become worthy leaders of tomorrow.

If everyone is educated who will perform the so-called low and menial jobs such as those of sweepers, 'dhobis' and so on. Do you think that education for all can solve the problems of our society?

Kalyani Das, Visva Bharati University, Kolkata

No job is menial or low. Education will enrich and enable people to perform the same job better, faster and cheaper.

Today even a small company when appointing an employee, demands basic education and some qualifying criteria. But in the Parliament we are electing so many people who are not well educated. Do you think this is correct? Why can't we define some educational eligibility conditions for the elected representatives?

Lakshmi P., BVB Engineering College

It is the responsibility of the electorate to elect the right candidate for leading the country. Mere educational qualification is no guarantee of performance. There have been cases where people with very little education have performed extremely well for the welfare of the people.

As a renowned scientist, statesman and a person of great spiritual knowledge, could you tell us about your vision of an ideal student?

Pranav P.K., Arya Central School

My vision of an ideal student is that: he is righteous; he adopts and follows the principle – let my winged days not be spent in vain; he excels in his studies; he is a good member of his family, school and society; he has the patience to persevere with his work till he achieves his goals; and is respectful to parents, elders and teachers.

*In these days when life is viewed as a rat-race by several
people, why don't we try to include philosophy comprising
ethical values and spiritual laws of success, as a core
subject right from schooling to higher education, along
with languages?*

S. Balasubrahmanyam, Indian Institute of Science, Bangalore

Education between the age of five to seventeen years
is a very important phase in character building of
children. This foundation is to be laid by the parents
and teachers. I would like to recall my student days in
St. Joseph's College, Trichy. We used to have a moral
science class taught by Rev. Father Rector. He was
the highest in the hierarchy of the Jesuit system. He
used to teach us for one hour every week about great
spiritual leaders, religious leaders, renowned scientists
and above all good human beings. I am convinced
that what I learnt in that class of moral science stands
by me even today. Teaching of such courses called
"Elevating Young Minds" in the schools and colleges
at least once in a week and discussing about great
personalities from Hinduism, Islam, Christianity and
other religions will have a positive influence on the
young minds. In addition, it can include discussion
on great human beings such as Confucius, Buddha,
St. Augustine, Kalifa Omar, Mahatma Gandhi,
Rabindra Nath Tagore, Einstein, Abraham Lincoln
and moral stories linked to our civilisational heritage.

*Education must lead
to the creation of
job-providers rather
than job-seekers*

Will our education system be able to get rid of
unemployment, terrorism, corruption and poverty?

Puneet, AITEC, Bangalore

This is possible by combination of education with
value system, religion transforming into spiritual
force, economic development in an integrated way
and this will lead to national development. We will
definitely get enlightened citizens in a nation of billion
people.

According to you, what are the qualities of a good
teacher?

Shantha, JSS Pre-University College, Nanjangud, Mysore

A good teacher is one who loves children and enjoys
teaching. He should be able to help average students
to improve their performance. He should treat
teaching as a mission, where he is not merely teaching
a student, but he is producing an enlightened citizen
who is going to make a difference to the country.

With networking facility now available almost at every home, is classroom education still relevant?

Swati Joshi, Mangalam DAV Public School, Adityanagar, Morak, Dist. Kota

Classroom teaching cannot be substituted by distance education. Both are complementary. The role of the teacher is vital up to secondary education. Tele-education can be used to enrich the content of higher education.

What type of education system do you view in your imagination of India 2020?

Nivedita, Coast Guard Public School, Daman

Primary education should focus on triggering the creativity of the children. Secondary education should provide the confidence and capabilities in children to start their own small enterprise or go for higher education or research. Institutions of higher education should become world-class centers of excellence and partners of industry.

What changes should be made in the present education system so that the students of science feel more enthusiastic about the study of science?

Huda Masood, Sr. Sec. School, Aligarh

Firstly, the simple beauty of logic in science should be explained to the students. Take the example of our human body. Science has revealed that the human body is made up of millions and millions of atoms. An average adult weighing 70 kilograms would have approximately 7×10^{27} atoms, that is, 7 followed by 27 zeros. For example, I am made up of 5.8×10^{27} atoms. These are further divided into 4.7×10^{27} hydrogen atoms, another 1.8×10^{27} oxygen atoms, and there are 47.5×10^{26} carbon atoms. The difference between one human being and another is determined by the sequencing of the atoms. Such beauty of science should be explained to the students. Secondly, we must have inspiring teachers in science. Thirdly, students must be exposed to the lives and work of great scientists, so that they can derive inspiration from them. Fourthly, the value of science must be emphasized by senior scientists.

Recently, I was reading the book titled The Big and the Small–From the Microcosm to the Macrocosm, written by Dr. G. Venkataraman. In this book, the author establishes a fascinating link between particles of physics and cosmology. I would like to narrate an incident from the book about Sir CV Raman.

Raman was in the first batch of Bharat Ratna Award winners. The award ceremony was to take place in the last week of January, soon after the Republic Day celebrations of 1954. The then President Dr. Rajendra Prasad wrote to Raman inviting him to be his personal guest in the Rashtrapati Bhavan, when he came to Delhi for the award ceremony. Raman wrote a polite letter, regretting his inability to do so. And he had a noble reason for his inability to attend the investiture ceremony. He explained to the President that he was guiding a Ph.D. student and that the thesis had to be submitted by the last day of January. The student was valiantly trying to wrap it up and Raman felt he had to be by the side of the research student to see that the thesis was finished, sign the thesis as the guide and then have it submitted. Here was a scientist who gave up the pomp of a glittering ceremony associated with the highest honour, because he felt that his duty required him to be by the side of the student. It is this character that truly builds science. Students must be encouraged to build such character.

Swami Vivekananda was always keenly interested in the development of youth. He was very stern and would say that we have to produce lions and not slaves. Sir, what change can you implement in our present educational system to produce lions out of our youth?

Lakshmi, Meerut

My idea of education is to bring out the creativity of the individual. I certainly do not want the education system to create lions, because lions are man-eaters!

Creating a Scientific Spirit

Science is the best boon God has bestowed upon mankind. Science with reasoning becomes the capital of society. In whatever field we work, be it science, technology, medicine, politics, policing, theology, religion or judiciary, we have to use science in the service of the common man whose well-being is central to all human knowledge and endeavour.

Science is all about asking questions and finding the right answers through hard work and research into laws of nature. It is a fascinating subject and students get attracted to science if there are scientific problems which trigger their curiosity, are practically relevant, and are beautiful to pursue; and the teachers are good role models. The solution to scientific problems is universal and does not depend on the country you live in because science and scientific pursuits are borderless.

With the advances in information technology, the world has shrunk and become a global village and networking of scientists is necessary to solve the complex real world problems. In ancient times, India was a preferred destination for learning and research in science and philosophy. But in the past few decades the scientist movement had been from the East to the West. Of late, we have again started seeing the trend of visits by scientists from the developed nations to India. We have to strive to make India a centre of excellence in science and research.

Please tell me, who was the first scientist in the world?

Devesh Ranjan, N.I.C., New Delhi

Science was born and survives only through questions. The whole foundation of science is questioning. And as parents and teachers well know, children are the source of unending questions. Hence, child is the first scientist.

Do we really need to view everything from a scientific viewpoint for proper understanding?

Dhruv Saxena, Lucknow

Yes. Science is the only way man can progress fast.

This universe is made beautiful by God. Why should we invent such devices which destroy its beauty?

Harshita Gupta, C.N.I. Girls Inter-College, Dehradun

The whole universe is constantly engaged in a cycle of creation and destruction. However, mankind has to ensure that the invention of technologies are used for the upliftment of mankind without destroying nature.

How can we create a scientific temper in Indian citizens?

Shikha Wadekar, Mumbai

Scientists should become "civic scientists" and ensure that the results of science reach the common man. If this is constantly done and the people see the impact of science on their day-to-day life, a scientific temper will definitely follow.

In your view what is science and technology?

Samarpan, Jammu

Science is the process of using one's brain to find answers to the phenomena around us and technology is the process of using science to develop ways to answer those questions.

What is the power of prayer in day–to–day life? Will faith in religion retard the growth of science?

Jayashree K., St. Theresa's College, Ernakulam

By prayer and work you can realise anything. There is no relationship between religion and growth of science.

In your book, "Wings of Fire", you have said that "science is inherently open-ended and exploratory while development is closed-loop." Could you explain what this means?

Remya John, St. Theresa's College, Ernakulam

Science is basic and can be applied to many situations. Development is for a particular item and has to be done with a specific boundary of performance, space, cost and time. Thus it becomes a closed-loop system.

Creating a Scientific Spirit   81

Science is simply about nature and the laws of nature. But science and technology is destroying the very beauty of nature. As we know that ozone is depleting and global warming is increasing. So I think that this is not the proper use of science and technology but misuse of it. What do you think about this?

Preeti Sharma, RPVV, Vasant Kunj, New Delhi

Science and technology leads to development and that in turn has at times damaged our environment. But let us not forget that the solutions to this problem will also be provided by science and technology.

Man is progressing fast in science and technology but simultaneously he is losing faith in God. Do you think faith in God is a hindrance in the path of progress?

Rani Satphale, Nav Bharat Vidyalaya, Nagpur

Most of the people who have excelled in science are believers of God. Whenever Einstein, who discovered $E=mc^2$, saw the galaxy and the stars, he would wonder about the miracle of the universe and its creator. Our Nobel laureate Dr C.V. Raman was inclined towards spirituality. Results will multiply manifold if we promote science and technology with a firm belief in God.

There are many shortcomings of science which have compelled people to question, is science a boon and a blessing or is it a bane and a curse. So, what are the ways to reduce these shortcomings?

Manisha, Oxford Sr. Sec. School, Delhi

Science is innocent. It is certainly not a bane. It is how science is used by man that makes it a blessing or a curse. For example nuclear energy can be used for generation of electricity and also for making bombs. Fertilizers can be used in agriculture to improve the yield while the same chemicals can also be used in chemical weapons.

Science leads to technology and the leaders in a society decide how to use that technology.

Curiosity is the foundation for creativity and that along with a questioning mind will lead to the creation of scientific temperament

Which is the best way to bring about an affirmative scientific revolution in India?

Mankodi Pratiti, Shri Lal Bahadur Shastri Boys Vidyalaya, Rajkot

The benefits of science and technology must reach the common man, especially in rural India. This is what is being planned through PURA (Provision of Urban Amenities to Rural Areas). Efforts must also be made to promote science education in regional languages.

What in your mind are the three or four key things that would help India become a leader in making original contributions to technology?

Vikalpa: The Journal for Decision Makers, IIM Ahmedabad

We have to give the highest priority to :

- Education in basic science and applied science as this would help reduce future technology gaps

- Development of high-yield variety seeds to enhance our average agricultural yield by at least 3 to 4 times

- Technologies relating to solar power production particularly development of high efficiency photovoltaic cell using Carbon Nano Tube

- Work on convergence technology of information, communication and biotechnology. This will bring about a revolution both in information technology and medical technology.

Poverty is the biggest challenge in India. Can science be used to reduce or altogether banish poverty?

Mallika, RPVV, Suraj Mal Vihar, Faridabad

Indeed poverty is our biggest challenge. Science is helping reduce poverty in our nation. For example, information and communications technology has helped bring connectivity to many of our remote areas and remote sensing technology is helping farmers in many ways.

Do you support 'terra-farming' of Mars for eventual human colonisation?

B. Anuradha, BEL, Bangalore

Planet earth has a population of six billion people, which is expected to increase to eight billion by 2020. This will lead to two problems, one will be the reduced availability of precious metals such as titanium, tungsten, molybdenum and even the conventional materials. Also, the per capita living space will be reduced. To counter this situation, we need space-mining. This could be done on the moon, which is in between Mars and earth. Mars will be the habitat and moon will be the factory having zero gravity. Terra-farming will be required to make Mars fit for human habitat.

Whom should we have more faith in
– God or science?

Rajvir Desai, Bhopal

God and science both take us
towards the truth and reality
of life. God is important for
spirituality and science is important
for material progress. Both are
important in life.

How can we enhance scientific aptitude in our children?

Poonam Gautam, Pune University, Pune

We have to allow children to ask questions and we should have the patience to answer them satisfactorily. We should not stop them from asking questions. Curiosity is the foundation for creativity and that along with a questioning mind will lead to the creation of scientific temperament.

Since you have worked as a scientist for a long time and have been a leader of a research organisation, I want to ask, what kind of organisational policies, practices, rewards and culture tend to encourage or motivate research scientists? What are the important lessons for managing a research and development unit? What are the pitfalls?

Neelima S., Indian Institute of Science, Bangalore

For success in research and development we should have an organisational policy of promoting scientific temper among the scientists, openness of communication, tolerance to criticism, team work, collective problem solving and continuous improvement in performance. The organisational practice should be flexible, able to change with time and promote thinking and creativity. The reward system must be based on critical evaluation of performance and merit and the culture should be such which nurtures the feeling that nothing in science and technology is impossible.

Why have machines taken over human emotions and what is the remedy for this?

Binnie Arora, DAV Institute of Engineering and Technology
Jalandhar

If you mean that dynamics of our life are being electronically governed from morning to night through e-mail, internet, cyber tools, TV, computer, laptops, mobile telephone, I would like to state the following: It is the experience of many that all these tools assist in enlarging the knowledge base and making our actions more efficient. But at no time can we allow computers to be our masters and nor is that possible, since human creativity will always be superior to machine intelligence.

What will be our future after being a scientist, as it takes a lot of years for a person to get profits and sometimes his work is recognised only after his death?

Anita Jain, New State Academy, Delhi

Those who take up a scientific career and do research in pure science are not attracted by profits but by the challenge of science and their passion for it.

What is your message for the budding engineers of tomorrow?

Thomas Antony, TocH Institute of Science and Technology, Arakkunnam

At the time of starting their career, engineers should take this oath :

- Engineering and technology is a lifetime mission. I will work hard and succeed

- Wherever I am, I will always work with the thought : What process or product can I innovate, invent or discover

- I will always remember that "Let not my winged days be spent in vain"

- I realise I have to set a great technological goal that will lead me to aim high, work hard and persevere to realise the aim

- My greatest friends will be great scientific and technological minds, good teachers and good books

- I firmly believe that no problem can defeat me; I will become the captain of the problem, defeat the problem and succeed

- I will work for removing the problems faced by planet earth in the areas of water, energy, habitat, waste management and environment through the application of science and technology

- My national flag flies in my heart and I will bring glory to my nation.

Does science prove the existence of God or does science prove the non-existence of God?

Deepak Bhandare, Aurangabad School, Aurangabad

Through science we have been able to understand our planet earth and the entire galaxy the Milky Way. We are also aware of the existence of many stars and the galaxies in this universe. When we look at the new discoveries taking place every day we realise that we are yet to understand nature fully. There are many secrets hidden from us. Also we are aware that all the planets and galaxies in the universe are in dynamic equilibrium through an external force.

What is that force?

That is what I call as God.

Harnessing the Spirit of Youth

India is poised on the brink of transforming itself into a developed nation. The prime resource through which this transformation is possible is the 540 million youth who are below the age of twenty-five.

Children and youth are the picture of a nation's future. They are our hope for tomorrow. If their energies are properly channellised, they will unleash a momentum that would propel the nation on the fast track to development. We need to carefully nurture this vast and precious human capital by making it a focal point of our planning and development process. Encompassing the needs, rights and expectations of youth to the centre stage of development should be our priority.

Every child born in the nation should be allowed to blossom. It is particularly important to provide extra care and facilities to the children including those who are not fortunate to have their families to look after them.

My interactions with children in India and in other nations reveal that aspirations of the young are the same, that is, to live in a peaceful, prosperous and secure nation. All of them are looking for challenging missions, good role models and leaders who can be their guiding spirit. A combination of knowledge, enthusiasm and hard work of the youth is a great dynamic fire for transforming the nation. If India is to become developed by 2020, it will do so only be riding on the shoulders of the young.

You have a great attachment towards children. What makes you so attached to them? Is there some incident which has made you like this?

Aditya Ramesh, Kendriya Vidyalaya, Kochi

Young people have dreams and questioning minds, and with your nobility, curiosity, commitment, sincerity and concern for making the country great you can be moulded to become great.

Spirit of India

What are the special qualities in today's children and
how do you compare them with children of your time?

Yogesh Patel, Kerala People's Education School, Bhavnagar

I find that today's children are more inquisitive and
they want fast results. They have great ambitions
and aspirations. Also, present-day children are more
intelligent.

How should the youth equip themselves to make our
country achieve your vision of a developed India by
2020?

Andleeb Mirza, Unity College, Lucknow

Vision 2020 is not my mission. It is the mission of
the country. And each one of you can help achieve
the vision by excelling in your education. That will
give the nation the best doctors, best engineers,
best political leaders, best entrepreneurs and best
human beings. Apart from that, you can improve the
environment by planting five trees in the area around
your home or school. You can go to the rural villages
of your state during your vacations and teach atleast
five persons, who cannot read and write, particularly
the women.

I find that today's children are more inquisitive and they want fast results. They have great ambitions and aspirations

What do you think needs to be done to inculcate a sense of patriotism and service–mindedness amongst youngsters?

B.V. Roopa, BEL, Bangalore

The problem is not with children; it is with parents and teachers. Children are patriotic, but parents and grown-ups have to change their attitude towards the nation. If parents love the nation, they will work hard to preserve our civilisational heritage, and the children will automatically follow.

What kind of future do you foresee for the Indian youth?

Mueen Farooq Hakak, St. George College, Mussoorie

We have 540 million young people in our country. This is our core strength. They should contribute to transforming India into a developed nation. They should study well and excel. Entrepreneurship training should become part of their education. They should all aim to become employment generators rather than employment seekers. Great responsibilities are waiting for you, such as networking of rivers, execution of PURA, and above all transforming India into a developed nation. Every action that you do, you have to keep in mind our major mission of transforming India into a developed nation.

The youth today aim for a high salary with material benefits, they work for sixteen to eighteen hours, earn and spend lakhs and still are unhappy. What is your advice to those youngsters?

Jane Mary, Jubilee Mission Medical College
& Research Institute, Thrissur

You have to cultivate contentment. Happiness cannot come purely from money. Happiness needs satisfaction in work, satisfaction in relationships, satisfaction in contribution and above all giving back to the society more than what we have taken.

How can politics be made more respectable so that the younger generation feels attracted towards it? What are the skills that we need to develop to become good politicians and leaders?

Nikil Isaac Manohar, St. Britto's Academy, Chennai

The political system of a democratic nation provides vision for the nation and also focuses on the national development and executes in the form of government through the advice of the legislature. How do we ensure respect for the politics? The political system is equal to "political politics" and "developmental politics." The greater the quotient of developmental politics, the greater the respect that it will command. The younger generation must focus on developmental politics to make their mark as good politicians.

104   Spirit of India

With increasing parental and teacher pressure, burden of increased amount of syllabus, tension and most of all an inferior feeling in society, if we take admission in pure science, do you think we can achieve the dream of India?

P. Aruna, Bangalore

The most successful people are those who select the subject and task for which they have the aptitude, regardless of the opinion of other people.

Please give some message of inspiration to all of us.

Jyoti, D.A.V. School, Chandigarh

I have a message for the youth of our country. All the youth should have indomitable spirit. Indomitable spirit has two components. First, you should have an aim and then work hard for it. Second, while working you will definitely encounter some problems. In those circumstances, do not allow problems to become your master, instead you should become master of the problems, defeat them and succeed. Fortunately, our nation has a great resource of young population. Ignited minds of the young are the greatest resource compared to any other resource. When ignited minds work and perform with indomitable spirit, a prosperous, happy and safe India is assured.

Spirit of India

I am an eleven year old girl. How can I contribute in solving the nation's problems?

Ratakshi, DPS Ibtida Shiksha Kendra

Your first job is to study well and excel in studies. If you have time during holidays, you can teach two people who cannot read and write. You can plant two trees in your neighbourhood or school and nurture them. You can prevent wastage of water and energy. You can help your family members to keep the surrounding environment clean and green.

In the present era, communal harmony and secularism are vital to the progress of the country but unfortunately they are taking a backseat. How can we, students of the new generation, create a change in the mindset and environment?

Minu Rosamma, Joseph MET Public School, Perumbavoor

First, you should become enlightened citizens. Next, you should work for unity of minds among all Indians. When everyone is treated equally without discrimination, unity of minds will certainly be achieved. The principle is love everyone, help everyone, create an attitude of give, give and give.

Work with integrity and succeed with integrity —should be the motto of your life. That is the only way that society as a whole can progress with peace and harmony

If we students with a deep sense of patriotism try to enter politics how can we compete with and win against people with criminal backgrounds?

Satya Gowri, Osmania Medical College, Hyderabad

Recently, I have noticed that citizens are becoming more aware of developmental issues and development performance has become the criteria for electing candidates or the party. I am sure very soon the Indian electorate will fully recognise the need for patriotic political leaders who will concentrate more on development of the state and the nation. Also remember that you need to have courage :

Courage to think different

Courage to invent

Courage to travel on an unexplored path

Courage to discover the impossible

Courage to combat the problems and succeed.

You have to pledge that as a youth of this nation, you will work with courage to achieve success in all the missions which you undertake.

What traits do we need to nurture to become future leaders of society?

Apoorva Dwivedi, National Institute of Technology, Hamirpur

You must have a vision and the passion to execute the vision. You must take decisions courageously, you must know how to manage failure and success and there must be nobility in management. And above all you must work with integrity and succeed with integrity.

Today's youth is at the crossroads. There are four value systems which prevail. Values given by our ancestors, values given by our parents, values given by our politicians and values given by our teachers. Kindly advise us on which value system we should follow.

Akshat, Apeejay School, Noida

There is nothing like four value systems. Values are universal and common to all whether it is righteousness, selflessness, attitude of giving, transparency and treating everyone alike. These are the values that one must cultivate and follow.

What is the reason for your reaching out to children and youth? Is it to convey the message that India should become a developed country?

Stephanie, Connecticut College, USA

Children are innovative and creative and are always asking questions. They are the future of India.

*55 per cent of the Indian population comprises of the
youth and we all believe in the energy of the youth. My
question is - what is the role of the youth of India in
active politics?*

Tushar Katyayan, Siddaganga Institute of Technology, Tumkur

The youth have to exercise their vote to ensure
the success of those candidates who focus on the
development of the nation. Educating people about
the right and wrong candidate should be an important
mission for the youth. So far I have met over five
million youth and in each forum I have asked, how
many people will join politics? The number who
want to join politics is slowly increasing. I would like
to share with you some of the very typical answers
I got in response to my question – why do you want
to join politics? A girl from Jalandhar said that her
main aim in joining politics was to remove casteism
in the country. A girl from Lucknow said that she
would promote the vision of the nation and transform
the vision into missions and projects for time-bound
development of the nation.

Harnessing the Spirit of Youth   113

What is your opinion about the present generation of Indian youth and professionals?

Sujith Varghese Abraham, Trivandrum

I have met over five million youth in the last seven years and daily receive e-mails from many young people. They are all bubbling with enthusiasm. We should enable and empower them with education and a value system.

Who will you make the next President?

Neelkanth Patel, Tejas Vidyalaya, Vadodara

YOU, and you get ready !

Inculcating the Spirit of Success

The challenge in the mission of Developed India calls for a cohesive and focused effort of the young. A nation is great because of the way its people think. Particularly the young population of India must have a big aim; small aim is a crime. Though the present academic system may give students a lot of workload, it should not prevent them from dreaming.

Encourage everyone to dream for themselves. Unless people have dreams they will not be motivated to attain them. Slowly, you will find that, with proper effort, dreams will transform into thoughts and with effort and labour, these thoughts can be transformed into action. Success is possible only when we have a commitment to action. This 'dream-thought-action' philosophy is what I would like to be inculcated in each and every Indian.

As President and earlier as a scientist, life has taught me the importance of three qualities—knowledge, sweat and perseverance.

Our country has a very bright future, and all of us especially the children, who are the leaders of tomorrow have to work hard. The vision of a developed India will not come on its own. It will not be gifted to us by someone but we have to work and work hard to achieve the goals which we have set for ourselves. It is only through sweat and toil that we will be able to make India stand proudly among the comity of developed nations.

Should a person fulfil her own dreams or the expectations that others have from her?

Lipsa Hebram, Bhubneswar, Orissa

One's own dream has to be one's goal in life. One should do what one likes to do.

Which principles do you think are essential for a successful life?

Sijin Joy, St. Joseph Co-ed School, Bhopal

Acquisition of relevant knowledge, inculcating creativity, following the righteous path in all aspects of life and having the courage to follow your own dream will help you become successful.

How can I develop into an ideal person?

Mithun and Ashley, Ramakrishna Mission School, Vijayawada

By associating with good books, good teachers, good human beings and good friends.

Are hardships in life a must to bring out the best in us?

Mythri M P, Mahajana Education Society, Mysore

To bring out the best in ourselves, we should love our task and work with passion and enthusiasm. Under these circumstances there is no hardship.

What was your ambition in life and have you achieved it?

Raj Dogra, Udhampur

In life no achievement is final. It is infinite. One continuously moves from one mission to another. Sometimes you succeed. Sometimes success eludes you but you continue to persevere and continue to move ahead with mission after mission. That is life.

Spirit of India

What ultimately is "life"? What is its essence? How should a human being interpret his life in order to live happily?

Varun Yadav, Osmania Medical College, Hyderabad

Essence of life is love and to treat everyone with love without discrimination. This will ensure that human life is happy. Assume that the average human life is about 27000 days. Each day is a miniature of our life. Make a garland with 27000 days by counting each day as a precious pearl. That means, you have to spend every day with the purpose of being useful to the society. You will find happiness comes to you by giving.

How necessary is it to be ethical, moral and spiritual in order to become a successful person?

Jennifer Jacob, St. Xavier's College, Mumbai

Work with integrity and succeed with integrity— should be the motto of your life. That is the only way that society as a whole can progress with peace and harmony.

Inculcating the Spirit of Success

Everybody has something to tell us. Some say we should be disciplined, some say we should study, we should be honest, hardworking and so on. All these are important – but what is the most important quality for a child?

Dharma Mehta, St. Francis School, Mumbai

The most important quality for a child is to be honest to himself or herself and have compassion towards others. This will lead you to become an enlightened citizen.

According to you, what is 'Achievement'?

Abhishek Shetty, Bangalore

That which gives happiness and fulfilment.

What is the secret of your success?

S. Sukanya, Lady Doak College, Madurai, Tamilnadu

Dream, sweat and perseverance. You must have a goal in your life. Work hard to achieve it. While doing work you will definitely encounter some problems but you should face them boldly and overcome the problem. If God is with us, who can be against us?

The most successful people are those who select the subject and task for which they have the aptitude

What is more necessary, the favour of fortune or hard work?

Joshi Bhoomi, Kotak Kanya Vinay Mandir, Rajkot

Hard work comes first. Fortune
will favour you if you are persistent
in hard work. There is a famous
saying, 'God helps those who help
themselves.'

Dream...dream...dream....But how do you convert dreams into reality? We all know about hard work, honesty, time management, etc. but how do you overcome the fear of failure? How do you build up confidence?

Pratik Kumar, Siddaganga Institute of Technology, Tumkur

Acquisition of knowledge will make you confident. We should not be afraid of failure. We should learn from every failure and apply the lessons we have learnt. This will help you succeed. Focussing attention on your task at hand will help remove laziness.

Scientists are said to have brilliant minds. What should we do to develop a brilliant mind in ourselves? What are the steps that we should follow to become a scientist?

Renu Kumari, SKV

Be inquisitive, ask questions and work hard, the rest will take care of itself.

When did you realise that you are a leader?

K. Spandana Reddy , Hyderabad

Leadership has to be recognised by others and not by me.

Inculcating the Spirit of Success

What are the achievements a man must strive for in order to be called successful?

Bobin Biswas, Kolkata

It varies from person to person. Anything which offers challenge and has not been achieved by others and if you are able to achieve it, I would call you a successful person.

Could you please give us a few tips on 'time management'?

Master Mohd. Ghazi, STS High School, Aligarh

As you all know, the Earth rotates on its own axis once in a day, that is once in twenty-four hours or 1440 minutes or 86400 seconds. Also the Earth orbits around the sun and it takes nearly one year to complete one orbit. With the completion of one rotation of Earth around the sun, your age increases by one year. Seconds, minutes, hours, days and years fly by and we have no control over it. The only thing that we can do, while time flies, is that we can navigate and use the time. Remember, "Let not thy winged days be spent in vain."

Do you believe in fate or 'karma'?

Anand Prakash, Saraswati Vidya Mandir, Munger

What you are today is fate.
Tomorrow will be decided by your
"*karma*" or the actions that you do
today.

What is the difference between dreaming and planning?

R. Sathiya Bama, Tarapore Loganathan Girls Hr. Sec. School, Chennai

Dreams have to result into having an aim and goal
in life. That goal in life motivates you to acquire
the necessary knowledge, work hard and persevere
to achieve what you have aimed for. Planning is the
mechanism which enables us to put our efforts into
realising our aim and goal.

*Life, as you once said, is a mixture of unsolved problems,
ambiguous victories and amorphous defeats. So what
should we do when we get discouraged in life?*

Akhil Radhakrishnan, MET Public School, Perumbavoor

You should never get discouraged in life. You have to
become the captain of the problem whenever it arises,
defeat the problem and succeed.

What according to you is required to become a good leader?

Lav Jain, SRM University, Kancheepuram

For becoming a good leader you have to cultivate the following characteristics: Curiosity, creativity, concentration, character, courage, charisma, commonsense, competence, and conviction.

You were the President of the country and yet you found time to attend so many functions. What does time management mean to you?

Vandana, Heera Public School

Time is precious. It is a resource over which you have no control. But you can navigate the time to do all the good things you want to do. This is what time management is all about.

We are constantly told that learning is a lifelong process. Yet, once we start working, we find it very difficult to keep pace with what is happening in our field. Please advise as to how we can keep learning throughout our lives.

Priya Gupta, Alliance Business School, Bangalore

Yes, learning is a lifelong process. When you start your career, and each time you encounter a new situation, try to find the most innovative way of addressing that situation instead of going along the beaten path. This will result in incremental knowledge creation. Such acquisition of knowledge leads to lifelong learning. In this process, unlearning is also a necessary type of learning.

How did you develop so much strength to fight all the odds in your life?

Shreya Surana, Jamnabai Narsee School, Mumbai

Strength is developed through the acquisition of knowledge and preparing for every eventuality.

It is really inspiring to hear great men speak but most of the great men are so inaccessible to the common man. Is there any way in which this problem can be solved?

Manjima Saikia, Kamala Nehru College, New Delhi

You can read and know about the thoughts of these great men through the books written by them, through the internet, and by asking about them from your teachers.

Your dream of India is to make it a developed country by 2020. But considering that we are in the clutches of corruption, extremism and mis-governance, all of which are increasing day by day, how can we still hold on that dream?

Pradeep P.S., Mar Ivanios College, Trivandrum

If the 540 million youth work with the spirit "I can do it", "we can do it" and "India can do it", nothing can stop India from becoming a developed country before 2020.

Inculcating the Spirit of Success   133

Time is precious. It is a resource over which you have no control. But you can navigate the time to do all the good things you want to do

Why do you like to follow strict discipline in everything you do?

Saiyami Takale, Sanskriti School, Pune

That is the only way to succeed.

How did you overcome your failures?

M. Shobana, Thiagaraja Polytechnic College, Salem

Persevere with greater dedication.

How important is creativity for achieving success in life?

D.Surya Kumar, Hari Ohm Matriculation School, Palayam

Creativity is vital for accomplishing things for which you would like to be remembered for.

You are an ideal man. Please give us your suggestions on how to become a good human being?

Abhilash Verma, Police Modern School, Etawah

Hard work and spirituality combined with scientific temper will make you a good human being.

In the present scenario, higher studies and research are available primarily to brilliant students. How can average students thrive and progress in such a competitive situation?

Atreyee Dasgupta, Visva Bharati University, Kolkata

As a first step you must remove the feeling from your mind that you are an average student. All students have certain unique strengths. Please recognise that strength. Concentrate and work hard. I am sure you will succeed and will be able to compete with confidence in your chosen field.

In today's world where only marks are considered as the mirror of our development and character, where does the person with principles stand?

Viswanathan Sangita S., Saint Mary's School, Rajkot

Marks are a mere indicator of the knowledge gained in a particular subject and it is not a measure of character. Good marks must be complemented by good moral values and behaviour for your development as a responsible citizen.

You have been closely connected with rocket launching and conquering the sky. What do you think is more meaningful whether to conquer the sky or conquer the minds?

Abhilash K., Mumbai

It has never been my ambition to conquer the sky or the human mind. My aim always is how to use the strength of each individual human being and the power of their minds for the progress of the nation.

The 'Kalam' Spirit

The human mind is a unique gift. Thinking should become our capital asset, no matter what the ups and downs we come across in our lives. Thinking is progress. Thinking leads to action. Knowledge without action is useless and irrelevant. Knowledge with action leads to creativity and brings prosperity.

Creativity has many dimensions such as inventions, discoveries and innovations. Creativity is the ability to imagine or invent something new by combining, changing or reapplying existing ideas. Creativity is an attitude to accept change and newness, a willingness to play with ideas and possiblities, a flexibility of outlook, the habit of enjoying the good while looking for ways to improve it. Creativity is a process to work hard and continually improve ideas and solutions by making gradual alterations and refinements. The most important aspect of creativity is seeing the same thing as everybody else, but thinking of something different.

There is no doubt that there is creativity in every mind but it calls for a concerted effort to ensure that it is expressed. Every mind is creative, every mind is inquisitive, and when children ask questions we must answer them. If this is done at a young age, creativity will be nourished and the nation will flourish.

Creativity will continue to be the forte of humankind and enormous computing power provided by technology would be the effective tool that the human mind will use to craft its plans to create a better world to live in.

What were your feelings when you became the President of India and whom did you remember at that time?

Parvati, Secunderabad

The confidence reposed in me by the people really moved me. I felt that I should not let them down, and I rededicated myself to work towards bringing unity of minds for achieving the vision of making India into a developed nation. I remembered my mother, father and teachers and all those who helped me in my different missions in life.

What was the difference you experienced as the President of India and as a scientist at DRDO (Defence Research and Development Organisation)?

Aashish, RPVV, Vasant Kunj, Delhi

In both posts one has had to put in hard work, in that sense there is no difference in the two posts.

How does it feel to be the Head of State of the world's largest democracy which constitutes one-sixth of the human race? Is it a crushing responsibility or a golden opportunity to contribute to policy making?

Surjeet Bakshi, Delhi Public School, Chandigarh

I feel great. Responsibility and contribution go together.

Coming from a background of science and technology and inspite of the sanctity that the office of the President of India has, were you really at home and comfortable being the President? I ask this because given the kind of contrast the people in parliament, with all their criminal records as essential qualification to reach the parliament have, over the people in the scientific environment, this must have perturbed you sometime or the other.

Vinayadeepak H.S., Indian Insitute of Science, Bangalore

With your question I am reminded of the famous Thirukkural stated by the poet-saint Tiruvalluvar 2200 years ago that, whatever may be the depth of the river or lake or pond, whatever may be the condition of the water, the lily flower always comes out and blossoms. Similarly, if there is a definite determination to achieve a goal even if it seems impossible to achieve, you will succeed.

What do you do to achieve the balance, composure and optimism that are so obvious in your life?

Jayati Doshi, The International School, Bangalore

I keep myself busy working on one task or the other.

What do you want people to remember you as, the President of our country or a scientist?

As a good human being.

145

Given a second chance what would you want to be
— the President of India or a 'veena' player, a musical
instrument you like to play?

Deepankar Padha, Naval Public School, New Delhi

Given a second chance I would like to be a teacher.
Before being elected the President I was a teacher
and after finishing my term I would like to return to
teaching.

During your tenure as the President of India, what was
the most difficult decision you took?

Mohd. Zia Ullah, Indian Institute of
Information Technology, Allahabad

The most difficult decision was returning 'The Office
of Profit Bill' to the Parliament. I sent it back and
approved it only after the Parliament appointed a
committee to study it.

From where did you get the inspiration to become an eminent scientist?

Smriti, Kendriya Vidyalaya, R.K. Puram, New Delhi

There were three people who inspired me in my life and who gave me a mission. The first was my school teacher in the fifth class in Rameswaram. His name was Sivasubramania Iyer. He gave me a mission in life to learn all about flying. The other person who inspired me in life was Prof. Satish Dhawan who taught me how not to let problems become your master and to work hard to achieve your goals. The other great person who inspired me was Dr Vikram Sarabhai, who taught me the importance of having a vision.

*During your childhood did you ever
think of holding such a high position?
If so, what was the role of your
self-effort in achieving it?*

Surakhi Balakrishnan, AICT, Amritapuri

Not at all.

Reaching this position was the
culmination of performance of
multiple tasks and it was sweat,
sweat, sweat all the way.

148   Spirit of India

*What were your feelings when you were honoured with
the Bharat Ratna? How can I also become a Bharat
Ratna?*

Ch.Sairam, Ramakrishna Mission School, Vijayawada

Among the many events in my life, getting the Bharat
Ratna was one just more event. You do not worry
about the Bharat Ratna. Just love every job you do,
keep working hard, be a giver, serve others as much
as possible, and you will be a happy and successful
person.

*The five years of your Presidentship were glorious and
eventful. What is that you miss the most after stepping
down from the Presidential post?*

*Anupama S. Amala Institute of Medical Sciences
Amala Nagar, Thrissur*

Nothing.

Even amidst the most hectic schedule and numerous problems, you always have a smile on your face. What is the 'mantra' behind this?

Malini Ajayan, Jubilee Mission Medical College & Research Institute, Thrissur

Living in the present, all the time.

The opinion of a scientist like you and the opinion of the President of India, are they similiar or do they differ on certain issues of your concern?

Swati Panda, Govt. Girls High School, Burla

My views of today have evolved out of my work in different organisations in different capacities. This evolution is the basis on which my present opinions are manifest on different issues.

If God appears before you, what request will you make to Him?

S. Arn Venkat Krishna, Alpha Group of Schools, Trichy

I will pray to Almighty God to bless my nation with hardworking and knowledgeable people who can make our nation economically developed.

What was your favourite subject in school and why?

Abhinav, Air Force School, Pathankot

Science was my favourite subject. It enabled me to understand how certain phenomena occur in nature.

Can you tell us any unforgettable event that happened in your childhood?

R. Aravindh, Chennai

I am reminded of my fifth class teacher Shri Sivasubramania Iyer. He taught us how birds fly through his lecture and also by showing real life example at the seashore of Rameswaram. It is an unforgettable event which is forever etched in my memory. It inspired me to take up the study of science.

Can you share with us that particular moment of your life when you felt that you had failed, but later on you regained your strength?

Princy, K.V. Foundation Day of Urivi Vikram Charitable Trust, Delhi

This happened when I went for an Indian Air Force interview where I was the ninth candidate and only eight people were selected. I was very disappointed at that time, but later when I came to Delhi, and an offer from DTP&A was waiting for me I was able to overcome my disappointment.

Under-developed minds normally create differences. Developed minds create visions and differences disappear

How do you look at your teachers who taught you? Whose influence has been instrumental in making you what you are today? Is it those, who taught you discipline or those who taught you to seek knowledge?

Kumari Smitha, Gulbarga

I remember my teachers with great reverence. My father was my first teacher who taught me discipline and values of life. Shri Sivasubramania Iyer, my elementary school teacher inspired me to take up Aeronautics. They were the first to influence me and who shaped my life.

156 Spirit of India

I am a student of class VI. What were you like when you were in class VI?

Samridh Singh, Delhi Public School, Noida

World War II was being fought when I was your age. It was a difficult time for our family at Rameswaram. Almost everything was scarce from food articles to clothes to household goods. Ours was a large joint family. The size of our family was five sons and five daughters and three of whom, my father and his two younger brothers had families. At any time there would be three cradles in my home. The environment in the home alternated with happiness and sadness. My grandmother and mother would manage this large contingent.

I would wake up at four in the morning, take a bath and go to my teacher Sri Swamiyar for learning mathematics. He was a unique teacher and would accept only five students for free tuition in a year. His condition was that the students had to take a bath before coming for tuition. My mother would get up before me, then wake me, help me bathe and get ready to go for the tuition. After the tuition I would come back at 5 a.m. and my father would be waiting to take me for 'Namaz' and for learning 'Koran Sharif' in the Arabic school. After that I would go to the Rameswaram Road Railway station, which was three kilometers away to collect newspapers. Since it was war time the Madras Dhanushkodi Mail would

The 'Kalam' Spirit   157 not stop at the station and the newspaper bundle would simply be thrown from the running train to the platform.

I would pick up the papers and run around Rameswaram and be the first one to distribute the newspapers in the town. After distributing the newspapers, I would come home at 8 and my mother would give me a simple breakfast. Since I was both studying and working I would get a special quota of food. After school would be over, in the evening again I would go around town to collect dues from my customers to whom I had given the newspaper in the morning.

You are at such a high post, but how are you able to live such a simple life?

Parth Patel, Delhi Public School, Ahmedabad

My needs are very few.

What has life taught you?

Reema. Helan, LV Prasad Eye Institute, Bhubaneswar

Life is a continuing stream. Each day is unique and each activity has its own challenges. We should learn to love our work and enjoy every moment of it.

As the President, how did you deal with illiterate Ministers some of whom also had a criminal background?

Anushrut, Sardar Patel Vidyalaya, New Delhi

India is a democratic country. We have to respect the decision of the electorate by giving due respect to every member who has been elected by the enlightened electorate.

How do you react to the fact that the richest man in the world is an Indian?

Subham Sinha, Ramakrishna Mission Vidyalaya, Narendrapur, Kolkata

Richness is not a sin. But what is important is bridging the gap between the rich and the poor. We have to uplift the millions Indian people who are living below the poverty line.

Which was the happiest moment, and the darkest hour,
of your life?

Eeshan Chakraborty, Ramakrishna Mission Vidyalaya,*
Narendrapur, Kolkata

Seeing the happiness of polio affected children
wearing the lightweight FRO and running and
jumping around made me extremely happy.

The passing away of my parents within three months
time, of course at the ripe age of 103 and 93, was the
darkest hour.

What according to you is more powerful, the strength of
an individual or the collective thought of the multitude?

Aishwarya Sivaraman, Sophia High School, Bangalore

The collective thought of channellised powerful minds
is the real strength.

Has being a member of the minority community ever proved to be an obstacle in your struggle towards achievements and success in life?

Halima Akhtar, Jamia Senior Secondary School, Delhi

Dear friend, I would like to recall the song from Pinocchio:

"When you wish upon a star
Makes no difference who you are
Anything your heart desires
Will come to you."

Do you take any advice before starting any new work or do you just do it?

Rajesh Bhatija, Jamnabai Narsee School, Mumbai

Experience is a great treasure and you should always draw from that treasure.

Why do you wear a blue shirt?

Harsh Bhatt, Fatima Convent School, Bhavnagar

Blue is the colour of the sky. I like the sky and its marvels.

Why do you have this hairstyle?

B. Pritika, Tirupur

The hair grows!

What is the special gift of God to you or the special bliss of God on you which we see as a flash on your face and in your work?

Aakriti, Prabhadara Girls High School, Muzaffarpur

The special gift for me were my parents. As they were spiritual souls, I drew inspiration from them. That is the gift and blessing of God to me.

Which phase of your life do you cherish the most? As a child? As a scientist? Or as a President?

T. Sreenath Chelladurai, J.S.S. Pharmacy College, Ooty

As a teacher.

There is a saying, "Behind every successful man there is a woman." But you are still a bachelor. What is the secret of your successful career?

Shri J. Shankar, Ph.D. Scholar, Jamia Milia, New Delhi

As I come from a joint family, my father, my mother, brothers, sisters and my entire family and the people of India are partners in my success.

What mischievous things did you do when you were in school?

Ritika Ojha, Air Force School, Pathankot

One day our Headmaster was teaching us geography. During the class, after observing us, he probably felt that some of us were not being very attentive. He told us that we should go climb a running train. I immediately replied that if we try to climb a running train, we will fall and get injured. On hearing this, he gave me a good bashing. What he actually meant was that when he is teaching we should focus on learning. But instead of understanding it that way I thought he was asking us to physically climb a moving train!

What do you like to do in your leisure time?

Monica Lamba, Army Public School, Udhampur

I listen to Carnatic music, both instrumental and vocal. I also spend my time reading and writing books and poems.

What is it that you like doing the most?

Kirtan Patel, Girdharnagar-Shahibaug High School, Ahmedabad

Talking and discussing with children and understanding their dreams.

Life is a continuing stream. Each day is unique and each activity has its own challenges. We should learn to love our work and enjoy every moment of it

Which was the happier day in your life—the day you became the President of India or the day you stepped down from the post?

Sagar Kumar, Jnanadeepa School, Javalli, Shimoga

Both days were the same for me. I went from teaching to become a President and then I came back to teaching.

In your autobiography you have written that "we are all born with a divine fire in us…our work should be to fill the world with its glow" and further you have described the ways through which you realised the divine fire within you. Can you teach us how we can find this divine fire within ourselves?

Shridhar, Mar Ivanios College, Trivandrum

Each one of you should create an aim for your life by asking yourself the question "What would I like to be remembered for?" This question will give you the right answer and the direction that you must follow. Having decided the direction, you must acquire relevant knowledge from all possible sources. Work hard and persevere on your path. When a problem arises, do not allow the problem to become your captain, instead you become the captain of the problem and overcome to problem. This way each small success will become a stepping stone for your next success.

What are you afraid of?

Kritika Agarwal, Sanskriti School, Pune

I am not afraid of anything. In 2006 I flew in a supersonic jet and as I got down someone immediately asked, were you not afraid? My answer was, dear friend, I was so busy in my flight and flight control systems operation that I did not have time to feel afraid.

If you had supernatural powers what would you like to do?

Priya Dingorkar, Sanskriti School, Pune

I do not believe in supernatural powers.

*Your tenure as the President of India was really
memorable. You sanctified the post, so to say. But what
happens after your tenure as President comes to an end.
Are there any role models for the youth today? The
youth have looked upon you as an icon, but now I feel
there is a spark missing in their life, please comment.*

Ku. Sindhu Anisha Gujjari, JSS Public School, SJCE Campus, Mysore

Each President brings certain core-competencies to
the post. I have studied the ten Presidents before me
and they have all contributed in their own way. This
process will continue.

*What do you see as the most important turning point in
your life?*

M.Sakthi, Thiagaraja Polytechnic College, Salem

The successful launch of the Satellite Launch Vehicle,
SLV-3.

We have learnt many things from you. Have you learnt anything from us students?

C. Chitra and V.Sathyapriya, Thiagaraja Polytechnic College, Salem

The importance of asking questions.

Honourable Sir, please narrate one decision or incident that caused immense satisfaction to you as President of India?

Blesson Mathew, Mercy Memorial School, Kanpur

Three things gave me immense satisfaction. Giving assent to the Right to Education Act. Taking care of an injured peacock which I found in the gardens of the Rashtrapati Bhawan and nursing it back to health till it was able to fly again. And marketing the India Vision 2020 to the government.

You were a scientist, then you were the President and now you are the former President. How has your role in contributing towards the growth of the country changed in these positions—as a scientist, as a President and as a former President?

Deepika, Kamla Nehru College, New Delhi

As a scientist, my contribution was towards enhancing the strength of the nation. I also worked with a team of specialists to draw a blueprint for a developed India by 2020.

As the President, I marketed the theme of developed India to all the stakeholders in the country.

After demitting the office of the President, I am engaged in teaching and building confidence among the youth and imbuing them with the spirit of, "I can do it", "we can do it" and that the "nation can do it".

What do you like more—science or children? And why?

Akhil, Jnanadeepa School, Javalli, Shimoga,

Both, because I see a scientist in every child.

Who do you love the most in the world after God?

Jerusha D. Teter,
Immaculate Heart of Mary's Matric Hr. Sec. School, Palayam

After God I love all the creations of God.

Which is your favourite game, and who is your favourite player?

K.S. Manjunath, Dharmapuri

Once my favourite game was badminton. Presently, I walk in my garden for more than an hour everyday. That gives me happiness.

What is the one technology, invention or discovery that has fascinated you the most?

Srivalli Soujanya, Hyderabad

Discovery of electricity is the most important event.

You were from a poor family, so why did you choose to study and not work?

Rishi Patel, Kendriya Vidyalaya, Rajkot

My parents and teachers were very supportive and I was encouraged to pursue my studies.

What do you eat for breakfast and what kind of food do you like?

Teju, Mount Abu

I am a vegetarian and I like all Indian dishes.

Spirit of India

You designed one missile, then what inspired you to design five more, when the need of the hour is peace?

Viplove, Army Public School, Udhampur

My team in ISRO (Indian Space Research Organisation) built India's first satellite launch vehicle and successfully launched it. The ISRO programme is completely directed towards national needs of the common man – such as building communication satellite, remote sensing satellite, meteorological satellite etc.

In DRDO (Defence Research and Development Organisation) I initiated the development of five missiles, which no other country would give us and so we needed to develop them ourselves.

Also, all our neighbours are equipping their borders with sophisticated weapons. India spends a small amount for defending the nation and by securing the nation, development activities will continue without any interruptions. What we spend on defence is to bring peace.

Which is your favourite book and why?

S. Niranjana Devi, Trichy

Lillian Eichler Watson's "Light from Many Lamps" is my favourite book. It provides courage, happiness and knowledge.

I would like to know that whom do you admire the most in this world? Were you a naughty child during your school days? I hope you will answer my simple questions.

Naina Gautam, St. Thomas College, Dehradun

Of course my parents. I always remember my school teacher who gave me the vision for my life. Since I studied during 1940s when caning was a normal practice in schools, naturally if you were naughty you were caned. I have also experienced that.

*If given a chance, what would you like
to change in the Indian government?*
Sheetal Mahapatre, Ahlcon International School, New Delhi

I would reduce the compartmen-
talisation in the ministries.
There would only be a few
ministries looking after economic
matters, defence, education and
employment generation. The rest
would be managed by the private
sector. In this way governance
would become easier and lead to
competitiveness.

What is the future goal of your life?
Catherine, J.S.S, Law College, Mysore

Seeing a smile on the faces of a
billion people.